In the Plague Year

In the Plague Year

poems

W.H. New

Rock's Mills Press
Oakville, Ontario
2021

Published by
Rock's Mills Press
www.rocksmillspress.com

Copyright © 2021 by W.H. New.
All rights reserved. No portion of this book may be reproduced in any form without permission from the publisher, except as permitted by law. For information, including permissions, contact us at customer.service@rocksmillspress.com.

For Peggy, with love

It was about the beginning of September, 1664, that I . . . heard . . . that the plague was returned again . . . . It mattered not from whence it came; but all agreed it was come . . . . [T]he following week . . the distemper was spread . . . . This was the beginning of May . . . people had still some hopes [and] . . . began to be easy. . . . [but then] they searched the houses and found that the plague was . . . spread every way, and that many died of it every day. So that now . . . it was no more to be concealed; nay, it quickly appeared that the infection had spread itself beyond all hopes of abatement . . . . [F]rom the first week in June the infection spread in a dreadful manner, and . . . all that could conceal their distempers did it, to prevent their neighbours shunning and refusing to converse with them, and also to prevent authority shutting up their houses; which, though it was not yet practised, yet was threatened, and people were extremely terrified at the thoughts of it.

Daniel Defoe, *A Journal of the Plague Year*, 1722

Contents

1. Glass walls *30 March 2020* — 1
2. Rules & inhalations *2 April 2020* — 2
3. Fear itself *4 April 2020* — 3
4. Questions *5 April 2020* — 4
5. Shelving aside *8 April 2020* — 5
6. Social shell *11 April 2020* — 7
7. Herd immunity *11 April 2020, later* — 8
8. Sourdough *after 11 April 2020* — 9
9. Calendar *19 April 2020* — 10
10. Inhaling *20 April 2020* — 11
11. Crowding *22 April 2020* — 12
12. Roots & leaves *23 April 2020* — 13
13. Tedium *28 April 2020* — 14
14. Please ring *30 April 2020* — 15
15. Finch *3 May 2020* — 17
16. Sweet spot *8 May 2020* — 18
17. Transition terms *14 May 2020* — 20
18. Qualifying *17 May 2020* — 21
19. Messaging *20 May 2020* — 22
20. Cartouches *24 May 2020* — 23
21. Back room elephants *31 May 2020* — 24
22. Counter collector *6–8 June 2020* — 25
23. Unintended consequences *15 June 2020* — 26
24. Auf Wiedersehen *20 March 1917–18 June 2020* — 27
25. Longest day *21 June 2020* — 28
26. Gibbous *27–28 June 2020* — 29
27. Up for the count? *11 July 2020* — 30
28. The day before Bastille Day *13 July 2020* — 31
29. Covid summer *28 July 2020* — 32
30. Mask theatre *31 July 2020* — 34
31. On the road *7 August 2020* — 36
32. Wave's progress *17 August 2020* — 38

33.	Vision 20–20 *20 August 2020*	39
34.	Testing *26 August 2020*	41
35.	Overture *5 September 2020*	42
36.	Uptick *14 September 2020*	44
37.	Signs *22 September 2020*	45
38.	Signs 2: Mirrorglass *1 October 2020*	46
39.	Numbers *3 October 2020*	47
40.	The animals we sing about now *11 October 2020*	48
41.	Coming soon *20 October 2020*	50
42.	Thirteen *Late October 2020*	52
43.	Wearing distance *6 November 2020*	54
44.	In the poppy field *11 November 2020*	56
45.	Transmission *14 November 2020*	58
46.	Other voices *26 November 2020*	60
47.	Suspended *1 December 2020*	61
48.	After-effects *6 December 2020*	63
49.	The ordinary *10 December 2020*	64
50.	Wintergarden *11 December 2020*	66
51.	Inside *17 December 2020*	67
52.	Twins *29 December 2020*	69
53.	Anecdotal evidence *3 January 2021*	70
54.	News of the plague *12 January 2021*	72
55.	*Hamamelis mollis, var. pallida* *20 January 2021*	74
56.	Carriers *28 January 2021*	75
57.	Waiting for the next shoe *5 February 2021*	76
58.	Ad in *14 February 2021*	77
59.	Sedimentary, my dear Watson *24 February 2021*	78
60.	Deciphering *2 March 2021*	79

ACKNOWLEDGMENTS   81

In the Plague Year

1. *30 March 2020*

Glass walls

We self-isolate, chatting with neighbours
at two metres, as though preparing for a duel;
we talk with grandchildren on FaceTime,
wave through a plate glass window,

and wear a calm face: *yes, we are well; we're
washing our hands; we have enough to eat; and
thank you we sleep safely* (though most of the night
we camouflage the shattering inside):

We are cautious, knowing how windows
allow us to see and warp what we see,
prism and prison, a carnival of mirrors—
but no one we know of is down—

In the greenhouse, in the first heat of spring,
I plant tomato seeds: they sprout, spread
their first wings, *we will get through*
I tell myself, *we will all get through—*

2. *2 April 2020*

Rules & inhalations

Every day we learn more about Covid19:
what it looks like magnified ten thousand
times or more, spiked and spherical:
a *bearded crown*, they say, *corona*:

they tell us how it travels, droplet by droplet,
and how it fastens to the bristles in the nose—
the barbels, our body's fierce screen against
the air we breathe, now become our enemy—

They give us rules: *Wash: Avoid others* ('like
the plague,' we murmur): *Do not touch your face*—
provoking the nose to twitch, the chin to summon
stroking, the corners of the eye to fill with crust:

the hands fly to the top of the head as though
just to scratch, but then they drift and wander,
a single fingernail running a wrinkle
across the face of order—

We shrink from touch: it is death, we hear,
to breathe the virus in, knowing it could be
there already, bearded, itching to expand,
or settling, stretching, beyond our reach—

3. *4 April 2020*

Fear itself

*Wash your hands. Repeat. Wash
your hands. The backs of them too.
Remember the knuckles, the nails.
It will take you 20 seconds.*

Do you recognize how long this is?
Longer than the first Wright airplane
lift in 1903. Longer than the quake
in San Francisco. Conception

can take less time. Or death.
There it is: that word you want to
wash away. What do you say instead?
Droplets in the air. Just the flu. Wuhan.

4. 5 April 2020

Questions

The media pester us with petty
questions, ones that have no answer.
Ones they know have no answer, or none
yet, but ask them anyway. *When will
the pandemic end? Why have Authorities
not ended it? Why don't they tell us
what they know we want to hear,
and if not now, then yesterday?*

People look for answers, find military
metaphors instead: *Front line, Join the fight,
This is a war—* Shall I join in? *To the
hoarders come the spoils, to the profiteers
the rhetoric of shame.* South of us, a friend
of a friend has gone to five gun stores
to buy Protection. All of them are sold
out. He is a pacifist, he says.

5. *8 April 2020*

Shelving aside

Tension grows:
you can feel it at the grocery store, even
during the OpenEarly hour when seniors
get first dibs at the overnight unstocked
shelves. The clerks and cashiers welcome us:
in the face of contagion they laugh, smile,
offer to help and wish us a good day:

but some of the customers,
especially those clearly under 65
(so not yet old enough to be here honestly)
are sweating venom—It's not simple
self-interest at work (*me-firstism,* clutch
and glower, the baby boom dis-ease),
it's fear: you can smell it.

Faux-elders: they glare through flannel-wraps
at anyone who's strayed into the aisle
they happen to occupy, whoever they may be:
neighbours, strangers, intruders, invaders
with plans to snatch *their* paper towels
and the last refined bag of white flour—
But who's to judge? Maybe they never knew

anything but disconnect and plenty.
Absence, for instance, or fathers at war.

                              And then
there's the Queen on the supermarket tv,
reading her Sunday crisis message,
'to people of all faiths, or none' (*now*
there's *a change)—We'll meet again.*

She's citing Vera Lynn, who's a hundred
and three this year: *Yes*, we said, remembering
the war savings stamps, the ration coupons,
the blackouts at home and the iodine tablets
at school. W*e'll meet again.*
Yes. We're already doing so, one by one,
by the empty macaroni shelves in the IGA.

6. *11 April 2020, Holy Saturday*

Social shell

More and more are wearing masks,
as if disguised: as if, being masked,
they will be paler, not seen:

(They flinch
if you so much as look their way)

Me, I find it hard not to seek others' eyes,
with no expectation except a glimmer
of shared space, a hint of what the bodies
hope to do:

(Withdrawal is their only gesture,
like oysters when the wrong fish nears)

Alone on the sidewalk, solitary
in the grocery store, I am become
the wrong fish:

(We are underwater
and we don't have gills:
some have been alone so long,
they're drowning)

7. *11 April 2020, later*

Herd immunity

People who live on another block
have taken to walking past us.

They avoid the sidewalk,
staying to the centre of the road instead,

striding, not shuffling,
somehow claiming automotive space

as theirs by right. Couples,
in boots and tanktops, swing close,

declaring their coupledom.
Children tag along. Twosomes

stray, six feet apart,
one on the sidewalk, one on the road,

their talk preceding them,
their separating after:

Cases, deaths, projection figures,
those unknown:

the banality of numbers,
the geometry of one—

8. *after 11 April 2020*

Sourdough

Our friend T. tells us she saw the need
and wanted to do something tangible,
so started making face masks from old
leotards and giving them to friends.

She's left two on our doorstep, in a paper
bag. Keeping apart. One is flowery,
the other dun. I assume the plain one's
for me. It's *the colour of baking powder*

biscuits, I say, thinking distantly of my
taste buds. The truth is this: there's
no yeast on grocery shelves these days,
or baking powder either. More people

kneading means fewer staples handy:
Authorities—maybe projecting—
say there's no problem with supply lines:
We're rising to the challenge.

9. *19 April 2020*

Calendar

Sunday today. Only an external marker
tells me this: no newspaper on the front
porch at 5 am— Other days I'm not sure
where in the week I am any more: days
blend, one to the next. Or the last.

Half the time we even eat the same meals
at dinner—not identical, but same:
No one visits, so leftovers return, maybe
red with tomato, a different pickle,
or grazed with a dash of turmeric.

We still eat together, and can face
the next day of this long siege, knowing
the threat and knowing we can survive
the threat—*believing*, not in some fey spirit
or king-sized animistic rapture,

but in what we find familiar,
and in what the newspapers tell us—
that half the world is starving
while droplet by droplet the virus
rampages like a desert storm.

And what else do we know—do I
repeat myself? Yes. I repeat myself.
We know what feeds us: that we can rely
on each other, that even in the whirlwind,
we can—and do—reach out to calm.

10. *20 April 2020*

Inhaling

Four-twenty: another week begins,
the smokers inhaling more, I'm told,
but can't be bothered checking.

Cloud cover: not related.

People itch to be outside, normal.
Walking in the rain.
And no rain falls.

Static.

A caller on the radio
says she's built an obstacle course
for her children:

Out of plastic.

Milk cartons, boxes, garden chairs
and four-foot poles: the children
leap across artificial chasms,

surmount peaks a mile high.

They run off energy, she says,
exhaling, but not quite hiding
the tiredness behind her eyes

I'm too far away to see—

11. *22 April 2020*

Crowding

We are preoccupied with the virus.
And yet the world does not stop:
water lines break, and outflow floods
main streets and urban yards:

Crowds mass into small spaces,
asking for safety to be sacrificed,
mistaking impulse for liberty,
infection for the bogeyman:

Madmen and fools barricade
themselves in square cubbyholes,
shooting to be shot after rupturing
whole neighbourhoods: They claim

the freedom to be free, but cannot
tolerate the isolation that would
save them: No-one can save them,
not from their own jammed nightmares.

12. *23 April 2020: Shakespeare's birthday*

Roots & leaves

The neighbours have started wearing isolation
as though it makes them invisible—they garden
in red pyjamas, pick up the paper in dun fatigues
and boxer shorts, polkadot preferred—

I get it—no point in shovelling deep
in pressed jeans: salons and barbershops
are still closed down, so shag is in,
or coming in, with grey roots—

We've built hedgerows
out of frayed air:
we talk of May's rough winds
and summer on the other side:

we cultivate old herbalists' wild remedies—
lungwort and feverfew,
liverleaf and speedwell—
and let the dandelions grow—

13. *28 April 2020*

Tedium

Tedium: another stage of pandemic
as we try to get used to isolation.
Or avoid getting used to it: people
talk of the 'new normal,' but this is
not normal, it's dangerously close
to nothingness.

Tedium: I think it's one of the strongest
elements omitted from the Periodic Table:
I don't know why it was left off, perhaps
something to do with its atomic weight
or number, the way it displaces joy.
With glumness. A conundrum.

Think of how it sucks energy out of
all the other lapsed elements —orpheum
and kettledrum, gymnasium and stadium:
some people have looked for a substitute—
pabulum, sugarplum, laudanum and
martyrdom: but none satisfies.

Tedium. It's the failure to dream
of something better than the flimflam
nothingness of back lanes—elysium,
for instance, a second honeymoon, alive
and well, and elemental. And empathy,
maximum strength, the colour of fresh air.

14. *30 April 2020*

Please ring

We've had a month of Sundays,
with more to come: Online and
on the radio, broadcasters talk
about *the new normal* as if it's
normal, and neighbours panic,
tolling the same thing: social

isolation: On the street they
cross themselves and swerve
away as if the rest of us were
toxic: we've become a threat,
red ants in the belfry, termites
in the chapel basement:

But look: how far you can see
from the tower, and how fresh
a lungful of air feels, even below
ground: this has nothing to do
with termites, and everything to do
with the truancy of traffic:

Gas is down to 69 cents a litre:
should I feel sorry for the oil
magnates? Or Mark this: W*hat
shall it profit a man* . . . if the world
becomes so small we cannot eat
or breathe in company?

The truckers are still hauling
food across the continent, grocers
still wheeling their apple barrows,
farmers still milking the cows:
we have time to be grateful still
for those who ring the changes:

15. *3 May 2020*

Finch

Where thunder bumbled, clouds now part
to let the cool sun through: lilacs
bloom again, mauve and white: the sound
of passing bells, the scent of spring:

Startling, every year, this inching season,
one day bitter, one day less, one day not
at all: the closing chords of Bach or Mozart,
Requiem beckoning understanding:

Not that the plague has gone: we still
twenty-second wash by caring count
and mask ourselves away: but now we
know the Covid better, fear contagion

less, affirm our friends and neighbours
more: we are apart together, on balconies,
in gardens: Alone a purple-breasted finch
is singing in the wind-assembled sky—

16. *8 May 2020, VE Day, 75th anniversary*

Sweet spot

The chief health officer talks this week
about waiting for the sweet spot—

I think of the ice cream shop of my childhood,
Fraser Street in 1945: a sundae, cascading
marshmallow, chocolate syrup, a single
maraschino: I hear the clink of a spoon
in a fluted glass—

But she's talking about something else,
something more akin to the strong centre
of a tennis racquet, mid-tournament,
points on the line and silver waiting—

She waves statistics, flourishes them
till they sound like cheering:

You have to know how to hear them,
and how to read the way they look:
like the downward arc of a sales report
in a flailing candy factory—but here,
the lower the curve the better, till a flat line
looks like life, and not flat-lining.

Looks like life, I say, renaming openness,
the chance to meet, if not yet shake hands
or hug or kiss or spoon: to taste the sweetness
of community, to gather with the grandchildren,
to see how much they've grown, not simply
gesture affection on FaceTime.

We are freer, if not yet free. And one day soon
we hope to be able to gather.

17. *14 May 2020*

Transition terms

Every day we listen for the latest news:
cases, deaths, restraints, recoveries, and
today we hear the first murmurs of
transition, the shut-down ending,
reopening about to begin. We don't agree
on what that means: is it release, or is it
restricted: what's the tone, the bar, the
scale? Caution has been the key word,
but I can almost hear the ground shift,
as if crowds are already gunning for
cacophony, and rushing hurrah—

Random memory: of a music teacher
playing a solitary note on the piano,
asking me to say what it is—*B-flat,
or A-sharp?* I can't answer: they
sound the same. But then she plays
two separate scales, one in the key of F,
single-flat and moody; the other in B,
five-sharp and flashy: and asks me again:
the note's the same, I say, but I hear it
pulsing differently, reverberating,
each against a setting of its own—

18. *17 May 2020*

Qualifying

It's the start of the beginning, I hear,
the message curious, ambiguous:

not pledging the old race picking up
where it left off—3, 2, 1—more like

a coach's reminder: runners need to flex
their legs before they overtax their lungs.

More promises follow. Shops will open—
some of them—and jobs will return—

with limits: two-metre distancing will stay
and masks, too—and schools will open next—

We're alert, abruptly: *Next* twitches us—
it's a portal, looming, like *Afterlife*—

we tense our backs, we stretch through
Ready Set as far as we can—our limbs

tune in for the single-shot *GO*—
but don't yet snap,

in case in the heat a false start lurches us
back to the line—

19. *20 May 2020*

Messaging

Rumours tunnel underground like crab grass,
long filaments of innuendo: *the virus isn't
real, a trick, incurable, the end of the world
is already here*—they spread like billy-o,
sprout as slurs, come up as dodder, plots,
conspiracies and blades of blame—

Heat, and then rain: scrub corners burgeon,
front gardens patch in weed, neighbours
mull, mutter, clip, edge, mow, do
anything to get outside the house, even
push the stroller, teach the kids to pedal,
walk the dogs—

The dogs are happy: I know the names of all
of them who walk their owners by: Daisy,
Lenny, Rosie, Spot— Disobeying the distance
rules, they pad up to me, sniff to see who else
I've talked with: I can tell them what I've heard,
but they know already not to pay attention
to what I say—

20. *24 May 2020*

Cartouches

Instant gratification
    We hear of *randomized clinical trials*, & against our better judgment hope for quick cures: knowing time is not our friend, & if we ever thought it was our servant, we were mistaken.

Throwaway
    Quackery thrives in a pandemic: it promises a refund to generations used to *discard*: 'Get us back to normal, fast,' they say, ignoring the sour echo, that what they call Normal is what got us here.

High
    We say *Shazam,* seeking fireworks & calm, momentary ways out— a somewhere beyond the virus & inept imagination—but cannot grasp it: the trafficking goes on, spent cartridges & magic thinking.

Traffic
    Noticing fewer cars on the road, we see the people walking there instead. Are we making connections yet, learning to value space over density: leaf and birdsong, quickened drinking water, air?

21. *31 May 2020*

Back room elephants

The opening-up: today it's on everyone's lips
(tomorrow uncertain): not a verb yet,
it's a giant noun, a frozen mastodon
the earth has just coughed up, all tusk and
bone, its scent and thunder undetermined,
ends and options under-known—

I hear people talking of toddlers
daring their first steps, of rosebuds
just about to bloom, of paragliders
on the edge of lift: no one mentions
tumble caterpillar fall: they're listening
for the archeologists, the ones who
whisper every day about bringing back
what used to roam alive—

22. 6-8 June 2020: D-Day and after

Counter collector

In June we read graphs daily, charts and log scales: Fenced inside
our community, we gather numbers, count infections, contagions,
incarcerations: and when we're told 'No new deaths today,'
I think I should be pleased: I want to get out, to the local farmers'
market: an early harvest is in, and I'm eager for spring greens:

With 96 others at Connaught Park, masked and distanced in the
seniors' line, I'm waiting for the opening bell, already savouring red
berries, chard, asparagus spears, small potatoes: the bins and bundles
of day labour: In a shuffling silence, I catch bits of a fractured
conversation: *Have we given up on gathering?* a voice asks:

Another answering *Not me: I'm here to shop at the white elephant
stall—I want an orange Dinky Toy, rare hockey card, antique map,
Limoges.* In front of me in the queue, a deaf man turns, gruffs
that he can't understand, saying *I'm trying to read the ripples
in their masks, but the eyes aren't matching the shapes of word*s.

All weekend, reality's been charging our fences, breaking our
distance rules, insisting we think again about what matters:
marchers protesting a different viral contagion: colour bars
that say some people don't count, biases that suffocate, violence
that shreds lives, tears. When the market finally opens,

I find I'm not ready for spring after all: the berries look green, the
lettuce leaves wilted. And when I hear *No new deaths today,* I'm
starting to pick up what's become normal, what we're not counting,
what's tabled, reduced to nil. I read the shape of doing nothing,
the lines we've drawn to live behind, and I choke on the words.

23. *15 June 2020*

Unintended consequences

I have been reading Dante this season,
spending much time in *Purgatorio*:.

the restless Shades know there's a ladder,
but cannot first give up their failures:

The city tells us that density kills,
but still builds on green spaces:

Nor do newspapers reassure, their auguries
a catalogue of downers: local poisons:

bleach, lye, fear, distrust:
people have begun to burn their hands:

isolation, want, carfentanyl, defeat:
overdose deaths have soared.

In a senseless world, traffic seems noiseless
and air clean: children's laughter still carries,

and roses in this relentless rain are flourishing:
they perfume the dangerous air.

24. *20 March 1917–18 June 2020*

Auf Wiedersehen

I did not think to remember her so soon,
Vera Lynn: nor see Dover's cliffs
in such pale shade:

Weave the air for her, listen,
the linnets weep with recognition—

25. *21 June 2020: solstice*

Longest day

There are days when I want to cast bones, unravel
the secrets of tired tea leaves, read the entrails
of old poems to look for dragons' lairs:

Grendel's mother in the board room, snarling
with the laughing cavaliers; Circe on the balcony,
signing *Help me* to the deaf man screaming;

Beelzebub on the outer deck, feigning still life
with figs and avocadoes; the Duke of Ferrara,
clothed, descending a staircase—

I'm asking *when will it end*, but only ambiguities
reply: *when can we love again*, and sly evasions
meet us in the ante-room; *will we get through*—

Daily, reporters pose these questions, showing us
violence, which gives violence glamour; reiterating
slurs, which gives malice cachet; badgering for *story*,

which blurs facts; pitching numbers, highlighting lies:
ogres are the viruses that riddle us, draw us too close,
attach to our lungs and cling. Are you ready for this?

There may be no vaccine. Breathe deep. The air
is warm, the pollen count is down, summertime
begins, and some of the dragons may be dozing—

26. *27–28 June 2020*

Gibbous

Read the moon. Only half a quarantine ago
the moon was new: now it waxes crescent,
gibbous still to come, then full, then half,
waning before the cycle starts again.

They told us on a Wednesday that we are
entering Phase Three. We're uncertain
what to expect, more openness perhaps,
more company, more caution too, we hope:

the threat is still with us, the border
not far away. I hear traffic speeding up
already, notice more accidents, honking,
blocked intersections. Overnight, Covid

breaks out again, this time at a strip club.
Phase: from *phasis,* the Latin for *appearance,*
or even *shine.* Compare the word *face,*
my dictionary says: See *phantom, fantasy.*

27. *11 July 2020*

Up for the count?

Sure enough: the numbers to the south stagger us. Ten
thousand a day—or more—in Texas, Florida, are down
with the virus. Dr. Fauci says it could be a hundred thousand
because many are not being officially counted.

Dr. Fauci is himself attacked for saying so, because
official numbers *are* being counted, under separate cover,
even if large counts *(officially)* do not exist. What does it
cost to make the extras disappear?

Ourselves, we've learned new words: *surge* and *spike*,
but do not trust them. They sound like carneys.
The hard sell. *Go ahead*, we say: *climb your alpine peak*:
behind the hill you climb is one that's higher.

Long ago, somewhere at the back of our minds,
we know we learned that the closed border's porous.
Maybe it was on the street or maybe on the gravel ground
at public school. Things could get worse.

28. *13 July 2020*

The day before Bastille Day

Tomorrow's a long way off, but we talk about it
anyway, as though it's already in reach:
it's the day we're back to normal,
the day we're free to do as we like,
the day the masks are down, the walls are down,
and we're all
equal—

Hah. Look what happened when they
stormed the Bastille.
Equal, brotherly, free?
Chopped the head off a monarch,
but left the reign of terror there instead.

Did only the rats and fleas
survive the plague?

I've been reading Heinlein this week—
Stranger in a Strange Land—
maybe the walls are already down:
maybe we're on holiday, gone for the
whole weekend, visiting a different planet:

and maybe we've taken distance with us:

maybe we exist just to be food
for microbes and viruses,
and we're just finding out
that we don't yet speak their language—

29. *28 July 2020*
    100 days since the first local outbreak

Covid summer

What happens to community
in a covid summer? It wants to stretch:
but after a boxed-in winter, the whole country
does more than flex, it heats up: fire, flood,
humidity, high winds—

a jogger mutters *Running alone's
just blisters with a dash of torment.*

We stay inside with the A/C on, or else
grumble, stress, dare the mosquitoes
and fling ourselves outdoors:

Some people listen too much to broadcasts
from the neighbours, borrow their language,
their starry hats, their striped entitlement buttons
and gather in party buses, chanting *Hoax, hoax*:

their words smell of fear, their own uncertainty
hatching divisiveness up close and online,
news broadcasts too often too crayoned by
cravings for story
and settling for gossip and attitude:

Anti-mask rallies break out like pustules,
crowds turn giddy,
distancing breaks down:

We're flat-footed.

What can't happen here, we say,
is already happening, the numbers clambering up again:
contagion. On the beaches. At the bar.
On the air.

30. *31 July 2020*

Mask theatre

Oh c'mon, it can't be all bad—stop wearing the gloomy hat
and pull some sunshine into play:

Things are pretty good, considering—compare Texas, say—
we eat, sleep, talk, kiss, remember:

the farmers' market's full of fresh food,
lines move quickly once they start,

and in the garden we can get together for a glass of wine,
a cake, a cup of tea: as long as we keep the numbers down.

It's that drum circle last weekend that has people stirred—
the one that turned Third Beach into a vector,

an anti-mask melee—and even that's cooled down.
Partly because of our sense of theatre, eh? Which is

where we live. Since then some wag's painted a picture
of Dr. Bonnie, right—looking stern—I mean *really* stern—

and raised it on a ten-foot pole in the middle of the beach.
Here's your lifeguard, it says. And what else—

maybe it's all implied. *I can help you, but I can't save you
from being unwise?* though what she openly says

is easier to hear: *Bend the curve, not the rules.*
And so we try. Most of us. You see people on the street

wearing illustrated masks now: totems, superheroes,
hockey team insignia—community commitment, I guess.

One couple last week even wore matching messages:
Be careful, flashes one. The other one? *Be kind.*

31. *7 August 2020*

On the road

Dr. Bonnie tells us to go outside, into the parks
and the warm weather, get out into fresh air
even if we don't know where to go
or where we're already going
or where we'll end up in the long run
even if it's only halfway home.

But *keep our distance*, sure,
so we have that to think about too.

And the fact that campgrounds are all full
till at least the schools go back.

Meaning we should go biking. For solitary
exercise. That's approved. Except
the bike lanes are packed.

And passing cars and rival runners and
random parkers and ambling time-travellers
are constantly crossing the line.

Yesterday a load of lumber on the back of a pickup
shifted on the highway, knocked a biker into the ER.
Good luck to him with the fresh air
and the broken bones.

*

Interviewed today,
the guy who operates the local bike shop
says there's been a run on bikes all over the city,
those that sell for under a thousand:
he says nothing's even on display right now
except the heavy steel ones, but people want
10-speed electrified.

I guess he knows we're all pedalling uphill
and hoping not to have to stop.

32. *17 August 2020*

Wave's progress

Ocean: wastewater grey, predictable
as fog when all we see is overcast
turned upside down: or sometimes in
summer light, bluebrittle, rippling green:

The summer sun these hot August days
misleads us: our certainties are grim,
uncertainties grimmer: burdened, we
try to mishear plague's progress:

How short the seasons are, how uncertain
what day it is: every moment's another
Monday, a rip tide unbidden, sweeping
our feet from under, tumbling:

Stress: pandemic all its own: an under-
tow of reaching up and drawing down,
repetition that spins out, stretches,
spreads, a sea of sameness: Statisticians

dream in numbers: count violent incidents
in ordinary homes, list borrowed conspiracies,
their charts a catalogue of online gossip,
billowing half-truths, seas of floating lies:

We're forgetting what we used to dream about
and think important: plastic straws and green
food, climate change and drinking water,
how ordinary life was poisoning the ocean:

33. *20 August 2020*

Vision 20–20

The teen running cash at the grocery check-out
greets me with a question, *How are you?*
Well, I answer, *and how are you?* It's more

than empty talk: it's safety. We smile, or at least
I think we smile: we have to guess through our
masks—we've learned to ignore the mouth

and listen to the voice, ignore the uniform
and watch the eyes, for brightness, the hint
of crinkle at the edges, the kind that displaces

any fret we may have been lingering on:
we could be asymptomatic of course, but
choose to trust, reading the eyes: they tell us

if we've gone numb, or if we still find pleasure
in the world, still remember friendship and
even count on it. I know my eyes are dimming,

so I do not know if I have met her before—but
I see in her what I see in other teens: resolve:
wanting to look steady and be happy, facing

hazard, inhaling doubt. She's about to go back
to school, she says, ringing up what I owe (for a
nectarine, Italian prunes, two pears, it's harvest

season), and wonders aloud how her classes will
manage viral distancing: it isn't a question: *I'll
manage*, she answers herself: *we'll all manage*,

*together: besides, it'll be good to see everyone,
we've a lot of things we want to figure out yet,
and we don't give up on spring just because of fall:*

34. *26 August 2020*

Testing

And yet
    this fortnight

Numbers
    up again

New norms
    a Second Wave

Distance
    so hard

Home truths
    silences

We've had
    to learn

Too early
    to say

Goodbye

35. *5 September 2020*

Overture

Over
    and over, people are asking how long will it
    last, will it keep going on, will the end
    ever come—how and when will it all be
Over—
    and over we go into one more month of gestures,
    two metres distance, the length of a sari silk:
    they call it a towel's length on Bondi Beach,
    a fathom in the fish and chip shop, a sound
    sequence of semitones: we're renaming
    space at a notional line: imagining edges
Over
    the sea and across the waves: are we furtively
    thinking our way through a score to the end of days,
    searching distance by ocean, beyond Beyond,
    asking for all being
Over—
    what are we hoping for: what light or darkness,
    secret under cover, what answer to the question
    that we haven't asked aloud—a four-leafed
    clover on a desert shore? an undertaking to
    prevail when all we know is the rumble left
Over
    after thunder's drummed by? the hang-
Over
    after the party's danced itself to sleep, lovers
    lost in the morning and rovers moving away,
    arguments shrill and soon to be wintering

Over?
    we are cautious, we are curious, we are caring
    and would be kind: we know we're not
Over
     it yet and the music is swelling and tense and
    no, it's just this: with each new measure
    we are trying not to be
Over
    whelmed—

36. *14 September 2020*

Uptick

Six months in, and after easing, *uptick* is the word
of the week. Contagion spreads, tensions thicken:
no one laughs at rumours of exposure on the nude
beach, though one reporter sniggers: people are
tripping over tossed needles and coils of barbed
wire—shouting *hoax* and calling masks the menace
of despots: Ivan the Terrible, ogres and trolls:

For lack of pickers, Jonathan apples are dropping
in the orchards and feeding bears: fir-eating moths
have occupied city streets: the desiccated flesh
of bright Australian oranges doesn't freshen us:
the supermarket's cargo ships have been delayed.

Rules of distance still apply, but disorder comes
hand in hand. Oregon forest fire smoke blows north,
ignores the border, chokes us daily. We hear about
a Greenland ice sheet calving, raising the ocean,
but cannot see. Someone's cutting cables, setting
piers ablaze, acting out their anger, anguish, gloom.
Space is political, the universe personal, like pain.

37. *22 September 2020*

Signs

NEWS ITEM: Over the weekend two champions of civil rights died: former Canadian Prime Minister John Turner, at 93, and U.S. Supreme Court Judge Ruth Bader Ginsburg, at 87. In years to come, will people value the personal freedoms they owe to these two, or will they set their liberties aside? Ginsburg called herself 'a belligerent optimist.' Perhaps it's a sign.

Yesterday a quiet rain cleared away the forest smoke:
neighbours broke free of their houses, heads in the air,
catching in their arms the scent of late-blooming roses.

I saw a man dancing, a woman embracing a maple tree,
an old couple holding hands as they climbed a hill, and
four children playing kick-the-ball beside a water park.

I try not to believe in auguries—so much impedes us:
the politics of rage, contagious fear, the sad smut
of bullying smoke, the solid bulk of invisible walls —

But look around: see those people in the park, peaceable
together; and see that table set for a family dinner, with
fresh bread, ice water, thoughtful talk about the phases

of the moon: *how to listen, how to clear the air, how to
remember, how to argue for the right to think again.*
I see promises, possibilities. Yes I know that heavier

rains will fall, and dense hedges still wrap KEEP OUT signs
around the rose garden. But today they don't seem
foreordained, and I feel like jumping—

38. *1 October 2020*

Signs 2: Mirrorglass

But lows follow highs, so joy doesn't last long:
we hear again of a second wave, climbing numbers,
lungs filling with infection, death threats, Zoom fatigue—

and people rejecting rules—less a prologue
to chaos than a sign of tiredness at home,
tiredness with masks, tiredness with repetition,

especially among the young, who want action,
elation, the closeness of party fun, a Tao of Now—
everything that metred social distances deny:

Why are we surprised? That is the way
of generations: to hear the what, dismiss the why—
For us old ones, Now is as awkward as long limbs

in a funhouse mirror, willing distortion to be the norm—
Fun is still inside us, waiting like hope to find room
beyond reflection, some Yin for an aging Yang.

Why do we worry quirkily about the young?
We still care about them, guardedly, longing for signs
of a happier future, one better than our own—

39. *3 October 2020*

Numbers

This week   the statisticians say
34 million   have caught the virus,
worldwide,   and 1 million died,

affecting   all   continents,
leaders   as well as ordinary
women and men,   among them:

Abinder: Añez: Bernier: Blanchet: Bolsonaro: Compaoré: Dutton: Giamattei: Hernández: Isaksen: Jahangiri: Johnson: Litzman: Lukashenko: Machar: Mantashe: Montero: Mika: Michustin: Onyeama: O'Toole: Pashinyan: Prince Charles: Prince Faisal: Prince Joachim: Quaiser: Salif Kébé: Tohow: Trudeau: Trump: Zingaretti: Zubiri:

Tallies are by definition   incomplete. Interim totals may   exceed 100%. Estimates   vary.

Everyone knows someone,   now:
a friend,   a friend of a friend,
perhaps even   a statistician:

40. *11 October 2020, Thanksgiving weekend*

The animals we sing about now

When it's all over
the grass will be green,
the sky as blue as it used to be,
unicorns will caper on the roof tiles
and all will be well, *when it's all over—*

We say we'll gather
when this is all over,
pairing common sense with intuition:
we'll shadow leopards through elephant grass,
defy fog and sunfire, ragged flood and winter's abysses:
time will tick again, we'll follow Scorpio and Capricorn,
Hydra, the bears and the fishes:
we won't know absence,
when this is all over—

> Passenger pigeons,
> sabre-tooth tigers,
> Amsterdam wigeons,
> Vilevol gliders—

When it's over, we say,
we'll embrace the world,
clearly, gladly, in leap, in flight:

or maybe like sloths in the tree of knowledge,
slow to say what we've all but learned,
our heads wrapped in creosote:
that truth is a leopard, always the same
and never: only what it will be, then,
when the grass is high
and we say it's over—

41. *20 October 2020*

Coming soon

By now we've memorized the long list of symptoms,
and check daily to see if something dire is coming on:
rash (check), cough (check), headache, sore throat,
chest pain (check), loss of taste and sense of smell,
fatigue (for sure), delirium—

this last one's most likely to pass unnoticed,
unless you count the way we keep asking
*can I still taste chocolate, do I still smell popcorn,
is that fresh bread, are those sweet peas?*—

Don't expect consistency here: we're human,
there's an election going on—we're being told
that a Second Wave is coming, maybe a Third,
and we're promised salvation—a vaccine—
Shangri-La? *Coming Soon*—

so we're starting to feel positive, looking forward
to what comes after. Yet we still sniff for a rat.
Too many scammers around, trying to sell us
ice skates and thin ice:

meaning we treat promises as white noise: the same
way we hear sound bites as BurmaShave signs—
so we could be missing some virtual Eden in the wake
of the plague: but that's an old story—
Tiring, this: keeping watch on the field mice,

looking past the rash of propaganda. Maybe we've
lost our taste for the politics of this pandemic. Maybe
we're numbed by statistics: the 40 million, for instance,
who we know have now tested positive.

Truth is, we don't know what's coming, besides winter.
Or when. So we listen as best we can, tempering
lullabies with ragtime. And if we put all those promises
on ice, maybe we're ahead of the game. Not
contagious. Not even asymptomatic. Hoping.

42. *18-30 October 2020*

Thirteen

Despite
Covid's
grip,
we celebrate
in small

One cake,
thirteen
candles

Flame
flowers
on a single
slice

Wishes
stem it:

We cannot sing,
so say the words
happy and
birthday

Laughter,
story,
ritual,
time

Our ages
will not
come again

Sharing
even
this short
moment:
joy

boundless

43. *6 November 2020*   [Sean Connery, 1930–2020]

Wearing distance

1.
Bond dead, bravado gone: and there goes Double-O-Seven's
coded guarantee: we took his simple answers to intricate grief
as life in mimicry, adventure—and now they're in hiding.

The Covid's eight months on, the enemy undercover,
invisible, virus in air—November: lockdown purgatory:
all we can do is stay calm, be kind, wear masks, wash hands—

enduring fogbanks and sullen rain, roadslick and rogue
lies, the season oozing through closed doors: Zoom fatigue—
Or else we don't. People camouflage their panic in weariness

and mute fury: flare up, break down, anger rising. Last
weekend's fireworks. Street parties teeming, mingling,
milling about, spreading contacts, scattering danger.

2.
And then the clearing up. The dailiness of aftermath we
only half-remember. One by one on Hallowe'en, eleven
costumed kids rapped at our door—superhero, sorcerer,

trickster, spook, secret agent, resplendent crow: they carried
ordinary flour-sacks, holding them open for candy and
recognition— We too were in disguise: wrapped in comic

masks and plastic gloves, wearing distance to keep the virus
at bay, yet hoping to bond. The kids were chipper, eyes alight,
laughter infectious, voices spellbinding. *Thank you*, they said,

as they capered down the stairs. The ground fog lifted,
the blue moon full. We wished each other a happy night,
and started all over, daring again to dance the dark.

44. *11 November 2020*   *Remembrance Day*

In the poppy field

Sometimes I feel as though I'm writing obituaries for a
lost year, for family, friends, friends of friends, for those
in care & those careless, for lost youth & wasted age.

Inside the last decades of my own century, I recognize many
already leaving theirs, giving up the cold celebrity of work
& love & resolution: this November, tolling their names:

those who once invited me into technicolour & onto the
stage, Rigg & von Sydow, Rhonda, Olivia, Dennehey, Brimley:
Osmond from *Leave it to Beaver,* Kirk from *Spartacus,*
taunts of expectation, fantasies of desire:

those who taught me to laugh, Jones of the Python, Reiner
& Bean: those who played with gusto, Meeker & Shack,
hockey's Pocket Rocket & baseball's Ford: & those who
made me see, Christo & the Amazing Randi:

those who asked me to listen, Little Richard, Trini Lopez,
Tutti Frutti, If I had a hammer, Neil Peart's drums, rock's
Van Halen, country's *Rogers,* Ellis Marsalis's jazz piano,
and silence, moody, the blues of Salome Bey:

those who urged me to think, about law & equality,
community, justice, race & gender & categories
of kindness, John Lewis, Helen Reddy, Shirley Douglas,
Alex Trebek: all gone in 2020:

Saying the names. Saying only some of the names. Saying that all our lives mean something, & remembering those whose names we don't know, those whose dedication took them into Covid danger, & the people in homes where care wasn't enough, & even those who didn't care or didn't care enough, making dying sound anonymous when the numbers are so steep: when we know in the poppy field each one of us is I:

45. *14 November 2020*

Transmission

And then, suddenly, it's here, the Second Wave
we've heard about—
                      no, not suddenly: it's been
coming, with winter, for a long time, and now
we're in it, abruptly aware, waking up to cold
sun after short days of stubborn rain:
                                      snow
is flying in Elk Valley and in all the mountain
passes: *We're not ready*, we say: we'd got lax,
electing to savour summer's easy overtures—
while across the country, fall Covid numbers
were rocketing:
                  thousands now are infected:
and if we do nothing, it'll get a lot worse.
Modelling predicts ten thousand infections
a day by mid-December (the statisticians are
working) and how many deaths, how many
more deaths—
                We are shut down: in this city
we are told to stay home, by ourselves, cocoon
for two weeks, then check again, as though it's
March all over: but it's Diwali, the season of
fireworks and family celebrations, shared food
suddenly online:

        People point out that bars
are still open, till ten (*Too early*, some shout),
and Christmas lights are spotting commercial
storefronts, both sides of the street grumbling
Too soon:
        On the radio news this morning
the reader briefs us with the latest numbers
and talks about stalled transference of power,
then goes on to tell us three schools are closing,
deaths by overdose are rising, snow tires are
required for those heading into the Interior,
and—as a concession?—a woman that he's
interviewing says *We will*
                      get through—

46. *26 November 2020*

Other voices

There are other voices. They tell stories
that some don't want to hear, stories
about the plexiglass of loss:

> *I could only wait outside—just touch the window*
> *when my father died: It isn't right: no one should*
> *have to die alone—*

Stories about pain, the way it narrows:

> *My mother's frail and there's not enough to eat—*
> *I can't sleep, for the worry—*

About relief, how it soothes, and burns:

> *Thank god for the foodbank, or my kids would*
> *starve, but the lines are long, it hurts to stand,*
> *and I can't carry much in the cold—*

Stories of the battering ram they call ego:

> *The smearing? No one should have to put up with*
> *people who spit in your face if you mention masks,*
> *and call it freedom. Freedom's*
>
> *not having to be ashamed.*

True stories: about living by upstairs rules:

> *I have no roof, no coat, no help, no money—*
> *What else are you saying I have to Get Through?*

47. *1 December 2020*

Suspended

Last month, research teams trumpeted three
vaccines. *At last,* people breathed. Then others
asked *So soon? Are they safe? What does 95%
effective mean? Who will get them?* Answer:

no one, not till next year. In the chill, people
put their masks back on and persevered.
I felt as though we'd been cast in a play—
maybe *Hamlet*—action at odds with stoppage.

Last week, walking Broadway, looking for
something I couldn't find, I kept expecting
whatever it was to show up in the next block,
or the one after—it never did. Instead,

the street talked, telling *Not yet* stories: a driver
honking because he had to wait to turn a corner,
a bundled pedestrian impassive in reply,
the liquor store open, the lighting store closed;

and *Already late*: thin blue masks unhooked and
cast aside: FOR LEASE signs on boarded windows:
a neon jungle gym proclaiming *Birthday Parties*
(door ajar, untenanted within): old men curled

in grubby hollows, half-wrapped in cardboard,
one of them clutching a stuffed monkey.
Scenarios. Act III, I say. Today. Alive.
On stage. With more of the play to come:

48. *6 December 2020*

After-effects

Most cases are mild,
recuperation measured
after two weeks down:

Others last six months
more: things smell funny
or not at all, dissolve in

Brainfog: memory loss,
shortness of breath,
itch, rash, clots, fatigue:

Lungs heaving, heart
skipping, seizure,
paralysis, death:

The virus keeps
tripping us: shadow
play.   Old photos

in the attic, unlabelled,
undated, lurk (lurch)
in the late afternoon:

49. *10 December 2020*

The ordinary

This winter month I've watched governments storm gingerly into pragmatism, opponents insist that unpredictability be rearranged, and some in the media stoke whatever looks like a fire pit:

*

We've bundled indoors, bridling. Full treatment for Covid still many weeks off. Carp and grouse.

*

Then I heard a man find ways to value delay: a chance to see what works in practice, what side-effects may harm us, over time. No shouting. No whining. No apologies. No sign of mercantile fervour or the leatherjacket arrogance of doubters and deniers.

*

Am I reading too much into the cold season? Hanukkah, Christmas, candles and the scent of fir? Is cool-headedness a new affability or just the fragile calm of a coal-eyed snowman?

*

Masks have come to seem routine this year, hand-washing,
practiced distance—we miss the blessing of touch—
but we've learned to honour care, which exists for us
as ours exists for others.

*Ignoring icefog then, the stumbles of friendship, and the raw
rhetoric of the careless, selfish, brassy, and vain, I begin to hope
in earnest, and for the first time in a while, I hear laughter,
impulsive and undisguised. I used to think it ordinary,
and now—shivering—I join in.*

50. *11 December 2020*

Wintergarden

Vaccine vials are due to arrive next week:
they'll need deep-freeze containers
to remain stable—minus 70
        What's that in real numbers?
        my neighbour asks:
        92, give or take—

I picture ice-houses sprouting up
like those silver monoliths that have
lately appeared, and then been disappeared—
anonymous columns of promise and mystery—
        diversion, until the vandals come
        with slogans and mauls,
        identifying what they don't see:

Think of being a stick:
summer eyes will make a metaphor of you,
turn you into wand cane baton plain pikestaff
without a howdy'-do—something suspect,
magical and musical and threatening—
        but in the wintergarden,
        you don't have to pretend:
        you just are:

One of the ironies of irony is that those
who need it most are least likely to hear it
for what it is: give-and-take, destabilizing play:
        Trying to amuse
        in trying times
        is dangerous—

51. *17 December 2020*

Inside

Vaccines are here, almost, two at least:
we're told they'll be delivered in an orderly
sequence—first to the front lines. Experts
mention speed and safety as well, and
messenger RNA, the sly cell calculus
that tailors proteins to recognize the virus
and fight it. We don't understand,
but spirits are eased, a little.

A few people are keen to edge up in the queue—
they say they'll toss their masks the moment
the needle goes in, mistaking injection for cure;
others think twice, hearing there'll be flu-like
symptoms for two days, and months before
herd immunity. One old man stands alone
on a corner ragging on about the word *adept* :
it once meant knowledgeable in the dark art
of alchemy. No one pays him much attention.

The rest of us are just disgruntled; we go indoors
and play scrabble, awaiting our turn—piling up
points when we follow the rules and place
our tiles in legitimate squares, or when we
invent a word and try to get away with it.
Ept, for example—the opposite of *inept*, we say,
wearing a straight face, doesn't everyone know?
Regruntle, to make happy again. *Ert*, at least alive.

Christmas Day may help, but it's going to be limited
and lonely: inactive, unreal. We wear solemnity,
sometimes secondhand, as though it's all we're
sure of. In these dark days, with the solstice close,
a diversion is what we need. Regruntling.
We may have to look for it inside.

52.   *29 December 2020*

Twins
(after reading 'The Pull of the Stars')

On the 14th, the night of the Geminids,
cloud cover blocked our view—

On the 21st, the solstice—all day on the edge
of sleet—rain pelted: the planets coursing

hundreds of millions of miles apart, the Great
Conjunction invisible behind a hill—

Light we can't see still kindles us: dark we can't
hold still drives us on. The virus mutates,

leaps out of Elsewhere: contagion spreads,
lockdown tightens, mink die—

We choose the stories we listen to: old-world
philosophers tell us we're born at once into

beauty and hardship, the twins of our being—
Elders among the Haida tell of the Snow Moon,

when Raven steals the light and gives it
to the people, releasing them from darkness:

On the 29th, clouds scatter, the moon in Capricorn
is full: rain hesitates: returns: the oceans urging

the earth to start again: Reading midnight, we
chase riddles, kin of the sea and the falling stars—

53. *3 January 2021*

Anecdotal evidence

The polar bear swim is cancelled: so are late-night parties and skating rinks, but plunging into the new year's an ice bath, Arctic, as cold as the melting floes though not as cold as the vaccines have to be. Pfizer, Moderna—a few people are getting them. Not the same as a cure, I mutter, to cold shoulders and deaf ears.

On the air, speaker after speaker talks about *Going forward, into the overnight, seeing the light at the end of the tunnel.* Cliché after cliché. Like a rattle of cars on an old train line. They're dangerous when we don't hear them.

*

I know. I was caught in a tunnel once, for real. Years ago. I was hiking alone along the Thompson River track when an unscheduled train sounded its horn behind me and I couldn't outrun the engine—I tossed my pack to the side, threw myself to the ground, covered eyes and ears and . . .

*

Deafening, the noise.

*

You'll call this anecdotal evidence, but I say it doesn't matter how short the tunnel is or how close we think we are to the light. We have a long way to run.

*

The virus mutated this winter. It's more contagious now. Dr. Bonnie's not talking railways or the Arctic icecap when she says *Be calm, be safe, be kind*: but she might as well be. We're in narrower straits than we seem to think, the light's farther away than we wish it were, the train's just as much a threat if it's only three cars long and we're too close.

*

Blood turns to ice, they say.

*

Old saws—they have their uses—they're anecdotes, distilled across time. Though evidently too chewed up to cover all bases.

*

The polar bears are getting hungry.

54. *12 January 2021*

News of the plague

Listing plagues is easy: *Bubonic, Covid, the Spanish flu*—
we tally them as though they're moths on a lit-up score-
board (Canada: 120 deaths a day *vs* US: one every 33
seconds), how often they return, what damage they do,
each separate person lost in the swarm:

It's what history teaches us to do, write them out:
    The half of Europe that the Black Death erased,
    they are anonymous:
    The mass of passengers in cholera-choked
    steerage, they 'died of being poor':
    The Niitsitapi, Stō:lō, Huron-Wendat, felled
    on first contact with smallpox and measles
(*seven generations it takes, to bring a language back,
children and elders, the world they hold in their voices*):

History others them all, until the plague appears to
victimize only those who are not us:
    We say 'the Spanish flu' although we could
    be saying Kansas:
    The alphabet infections (SARS, MERS, HIV),
    we say they come from somewhere else
    or happen to other people:
    'Childhood diseases' makes rubella sound
    innocent, and 'tropical diseases' makes
    Ebola seem remote:
Is this how we'll remember Covid? Or is it personal?

I think of a grandmother I never met, wondering
what might have been—guessing now that she died
of the Spanish flu, one of the fifty million, worldwide,
buried and gone. Invincible we are, or say we are:
living with absences we ache to understand.

55. *20 January 2021*

Hamamelis mollis, var. pallida

Dull winter limits us, wraps us in grey rain—
Pfizer supplies, already strained, stall,
and the virus hangs on: people are edgy:
We gave it a year, and now it's mutating?

Heads hooded, hands raw, dog-walkers
hurry through curt routines. One couple
strides by at 8 every day, never looking up
from paper coffee cups.

Elsewhere's no better, all avalanche and isolation,
bare variants of ice and curfew. Nothing
strays from the mean—
                                and then it does:

Overnight, the witch-hazel flares yellow:
passers-by stop, stare, wonder:
perhaps mistaking stamens for soft petals
or imagining a burst of seed.

Rumours tell of dowsers long ago
who could read the land with witch-hazel twigs,
divine how to find a wandering spring,
ask only for some augury of winter's end—

56. *28 January 2021*

Carriers

Nights are the best time on the road,
the long-haulers say: less traffic, least
rush, and after sunrise you can
catch some shut-eye in the big rig's cab.

Good to have a dog with you then,
for safety's sake, and decent company:
crack the window open, they can
catch the air—

But the doctors don't mean them,
when they say *long-haulers*:
they mean the people who can't shed the Covid
months after it's first hit them:
lungs gone, brain fog, fatigue:
heart won't pump enough oxygen,
not the way it's supposed to, into the blood.
Makes you think.

And now they're saying dogs can be carriers,
and likely need the vaccine as much as we do
if we're all going to last through the overnight:

Not sure where this'll end,
all the new mutations—

Just need to believe it'll turn out okay,
down the road, so we can all sleep better
and get safe to where we're going—

57. 5 February 2021

Waiting for the next shoe

The last ten minutes on a ferry—or the whole last hour
on a trans-Pacific flight—the last parcel of time
is always the longest:

This week, now vaccinations have begun,
none is available: time lengthens:
vaccine nationalism takes hold:

the pandemonium of rich countries, their fear
of doing without: it's not pretty, greed:
expedience rules, supply
vanishes:

García Márquez writes of a man who sells promises
and poisons: a man so preposterous he convinces
even astronomers to see the month of February
as 'nothing but a herd of invisible elephants'—

I look forward to Valentine's,
to beginning the Year of the Ox,
its stubborn honesty, its peaceful contradictions.

and in the meantime, wait:
listening for the rumble of animals,
thunder, the turnabout of stars—

58. *14 February 2021*

Ad in

Travel's been halted, vaccines postponed:
as though we're in fifth set, even, one point
away, match hanging on the next move:

air—

February's the longest month, snow
flattening the daffodils, harassing Saint
Valentine tossing hearts from his sleigh—

omens

and ice: The arduous Year of the Rat
is done, the Time of the cautious Ox
awake, waiting: delayed—

story in stone—

Seasoned eyes drawn to the shortest
moment, ears tuned to the faint
caveat of blood, breath, earth

and the river open—

59. *24 February 2021*

Sedimentary, my dear Watson

Much chatter this week has asked us each
to think about Mars and write a letter to our
future self: *Hi,* I begin, *They've just landed on
the red planet, to look for rocks and signs of life
in what may or may not be a dried-up lake bed,
but you'll know all this, unless Mars has already
been forgotten, so why am I bothering?*

Hard to answer that one. Because fifty years on,
my future self will be so ancient it'll be read
as a petroglyph? Because old stories have so far
always survived the plague? Because there'll
still be those who dream and those who fear to
dream and those who tell others every day to
get over themselves and eat their damn porridge?

Maybe because it's memory the astrophysicists
are looking for: the complicated sediments of time—
Flash Gordon and other supernovae, odysseys of
space and chronicles of wonder, childhood secrets,
adolescent fantasies, all those layers of metaphor
and computation that pass for adulthood—they're
how we tell ourselves we're real, and can live on—

60. *2 March 2021*

Deciphering

We're behaving today as if winter's over:
vaccines are almost here
        (*not yet, not yet*, still overcast)—
we've been given a date, a number to phone,
someone to count on, hope in hand—

Dog-walkers stride through the chilly
rain, their heads shrouded, umbrellas
angled, needles against the sky.

Numbers.
Stark.   Bare.
Like charcoal spars, windswept
in snow.

This time last year we hadn't logged
a lot of Covid deaths: 22,000 now.
South of us: half a million.
Worldwide: five times more.

People. Each person separate, each one alone.
Stripped of ledger, that's what *pandemic* means.
Rock, pitch, tumble.

Years ahead,
when we listen to stories in the firedark,
will tellers whisper Covid numbers, tally
clearcut and fall silent,
or will they trace riddles on old walking sticks,
sing of tending and the runes of neighbourhood,
weave amulets of love, reveal how frozen strangers
learned to read the quickening spell of rain?

Acknowledgments

I wish first to acknowledge the care and professional dedication provided by so many front-line workers during the onslaught of Covid19 in 2020 and after: medical personnel, food suppliers, teachers, service workers, cashiers, drivers, and many more; and especially I want to honour Dr. Bonnie Henry, the Chief Medical Officer of British Columbia, whose informed guidance and calm manner sustained us through the uneven course of the 2020-21 pandemic.

A number of public figures are mentioned by name in this book, but only in passing and in connection with the Covid19 pandemic—Dr. Anthony Fauci (the American physician who works with the World Health Organization), for example, and other newsmakers of 2020 (from Ruth Bader Ginsburg to Vera Lynn); further information about them is readily available in print media and online. The mention of Gabriel García Márquez in poem #57 alludes to his short story 'Blacamán the Good, Vendor of Miracles.'

Among the many works written about plagues—the Black Death, cholera, the Spanish Flu, and others—several in some measure influenced this book: Daniel Defoe's *A Journal of the Plague Year* (1722), which is cast as an eye-witness account of the 1665 plague in London (ostensibly by Defoe's uncle Henry Foe); Albert Camus's *The Plague* (1948; first published in 1947 as *La Peste*), set at the time of a cholera plague in Oran, which is often read as a warning about the rise of fascism; Emma Donoghue's *The Pull of the Stars* (2020), set in a maternity ward in Dublin at the time of the 1918 Spanish flu; and Maggie O'Farrell's *Hamnet and Judith* (2020), set in 1580 (when Shakespeare was writing the sonnets and *Hamlet*), which explores the deep, delicate, and often veiled connections between public face and personal trauma.

Even more importantly, friendship has been critical to the making of this collection, and I am grateful to my family and to the many friends whose letters, cards, emails, and Zoom meetings provided sustenance during this time. Thanks go to our friend Tara Shioya, for her homemade masks, delivered on the doorstep; to Ross Labrie, for an ongoing email conversation about poetry; to the 'Poetry Odysseans' for Zoom exchanges. Thank you also to Ron Smith, for his friendship, laughter, and invaluable responses to early drafts of many of the poems; and especially to Peggy New, for insights and suggestions that helped shape the whole manuscript, and for the love we share.

Poem #26, 'Gibbous,' appeared first in an issue of the *UBC Emeritus College Newsletter*, 3.2 (September 2020): 15.

Thanks also to David Stover, at Rock's Mills Press, for his care with this book.

About the Author

WILLIAM NEW was born in 1938 in Vancouver, British Columbia, the city where he currently lives. A graduate of the University of British Columbia and the University of Leeds, and a prize-winning teacher and writer, he taught at UBC for almost four decades. During this time he edited the journal *Canadian Literature* for seventeen years and taught a range of literary courses, focussing on Canada and the Commonwealth. Author and editor of some fifty books and several scores of essays and reviews, he was awarded the Royal Society of Canada's Lorne Pierce Medal in 2004. For his services to creative and critical writing he was named an Officer of the Order of Canada in 2006.

His books of history and literary commentary range from *Articulating West* (1972) to *Land Sliding* (1997), *A History of Canadian Literature* (2nd ed., 2003), and several studies of poetry, the short story, irony, and postcolonial narrative, as in *Dreams of Speech and Violence* (1987) and *Reading Mansfield and Metaphors of Form* (1999). Editor of the *Encyclopedia of Literature in Canada* (2002), he has also studied how the personal and the local affect political attitudes, as in *Borderlands* (1998) and *Grandchild of Empire* (2003).

William New's creative works include five books for children, from *Vanilla Gorilla* (1998) to the internationally honoured *The Year I Was Grounded* (2008); and his poetry collections range from *Science Lessons* (1996) to *Underwood Log* (2004, shortlisted for the Governor General's Award), *YVR* (2011, winner of the City of Vancouver Award), and *Neighbours* (2017).

www.ingramcontent.com/pod-product-compliance
Lightning Source LLC
Chambersburg PA
CBHW020913080526
44589CB00011B/569